The Translator

Dah

Transcendent Zero Press
Houston, Texas

Copyright © 2015 Dah

PUBLISHED BY TRANSCENDENT ZERO PRESS www.transcendentzeropress.org

All rights reserved. No part or parts of this book may be reproduced in any format, except for portions used in reviews, without the expressed written consent from the author or from the publisher.

ISBN-13:978-0692415252

ISBN-10: 0692415254

Printed in the United States of America

Library of Congress Control Number: 2015937009

Cover design by Dah
Cover layout and spine design by AJ Price Design

FIRST EDITION
Transcendent Zero Press

The Translator

Dah

Foreword

This fourth collection of poems by Dah, 'The Translator', reveals the subdued, watercolor melancholy of foggy harbor scenes, receding radiance of rugged canyons, and diverse personified winds.

Dah connects with nature's silence rather than downtown's cacophony. He listens to the trees, observes birds hovering over the rocky coast and meditates about the past and origins. He doesn't hurry to reach the turnpike of the sun-bleached future but tries to decipher the future's signs, translate its message, obscured by unfeeling winds.

A symbol of transience, fruitless striving and cosmic breath, Wind becomes one of the main characters in 'The Translator'. The aerial messenger handling invisible energies blows where it wills, reshapes and breaks apart scattered clouds and destinies and dampens once promising infatuations.

The woman occasionally appearing in Dah's poems is sometimes represented by her voice extending the narrator's reflections, sometimes sensuously sketched by varying chiaroscuros of her nakedness. All the while, fleeting blossoms of earthly romance are followed by emptiness, the existential loneliness of the narrator's Anima: "Sitting close to you I feel your unrelenting loneliness". "After the wind blew there was nothing, but a strand of your black hair". Sparks torn from campfire embers snap fragments of autumnal trees and disappear into the darkness. Permanence exists only in changeable seas, skies, winds, and the monotony of an inner soliloquy: "I have come to love the silence, the darkness, the end", which calls to mind a beautifully unsettling song about wandering stars.

The two characters other than the narrator's Anima and Animus are their aged and, in a way, more balanced versions: "the bent-over old man" who slowly rakes leaves "like an angel sweeping heaven" and the lean, greying woman at the marina, whose slow Tai-Chi circles and curves the narrator mimics:

Maybe this is the way to be content,
to create a stance of fearlessness at the gate to the one ending.

The narrator ponders human finiteness, remembers years of frequent funerals followed by ceaseless rains sufficient enough "even for the dead". He ponders the "staggering office workers" with "aching facial lines" and finds refuge in nature and fruitful solitude.

Introspective and guideless, Dah refutes the old saying that whoever watches the wind will not plant, whoever looks at the clouds will not reap:

My hands are the hands of a gardener
fresh with soil, sunlight and rain.

'The Translator' is abundant in all shades of existential melancholy. But at its core Dah's poetic impulse is stoic and bright:

My heart is bound to the coast,
to the cliffs that have mastered the edge,
to the sea that extends its directions,
to the sand that sails the wind

Elina Petrova
Houston, Texas
February 15th, 2015

for Eve

from whose Stillpoint it began

Table Of Contents

Proem

Journals — 15

Consideration

Fallen Sea Star — 19

Understand — 21

Hypnotize The Beast — 22

We Are Only Sleeping — 23

Some god — 24

Nocturne in d-flat minor — 26

Captivity — 27

The Translator — 29

Journey — 30

The Moon's Deep Wounds — 31

Origin — 33

Urgency — 34

Dust — 35

Spring, A Birthing Womb — 36

Wildcat Canyon — 38

When You Drown You Float — 40

Appearance — 41

Rattle — 43

Lead and Salt — 45

Kleptomaniac — 46

Yuba — 47

Worthy — 49

Time Is Nothing When It Is Dark — 50

Invisible — 52

Halos and Harps — 53

Sometimes Belief Needs A Telescope — 54

A Far-Flung Future — 55

The Sound Of Bones — 57

A Dream Held In A Mouth — 58

Observation, Recollection

Full Life In The Day Of A Poet — 61

Naked Cry — 62

Teachers — 63

Raven — 64

Sweeping Heaven — 65

Harbor Scene — 66

Rain #2 — 68

City Portrait — 70

Circle — 71

Scenes From Cedar Park — 72

The Bird Flew Off — 73

A Trumpet Blows The Blues — 74

Corrosion — 76

Morning's Mirror — 77

Departures: 1958–1964 — 78

Hymn — 79

Eulogy For Roses — 80

Ghost — 81

Going Coastal — 83

Sundown — 85

Nocturne — 86

Twelfth Installation — 87

In The Body Of A Daydream — 88

Embrace — 90

Mountains — 91

The Willowed Landscape — 92

Enchanted — 93

Solo Flight — 94

Gardener — 96

Queen — 97

Sun — 98

Never The Breeze — 99

Slow Drain — 100

Napa — 101

Banjo Birds and Circles — 102

Sardines Mesh and Scars — 103

Gate To The One Ending — 104

Nowhere To Be Found — 106

Coda

Earth — 109

Acknowledgements — 110

Author — 112

Books by Dah — 113

PROEM

We continue

to fill our journals

that become smudged maps

to our past

We travel back

to see what was heavy

and why we stopped carrying it

Consideration

Fallen Sea Star

The chilly North Pacific:
we build a fire for the moths,
a lamplight. Their wings, angry
with flames. Sky: dim and small.

In your standing stillness, you are
an old clock
that has run out of chimes.
The small hours of the past,
a fossil, a nerve. I hand you a flask.

You say: 'August is dying.
The stones are cold.' In your hand,
a dead sea star. Summer bronze
burned into your skin. Your eyes,
moist black pearls.

Along the horizon, dark fog
is an oil slick floating against the sky's
gray wall. Your silhouette, solitude,
the wind's nimble stitching of your hair.

You say: 'Memories are wounds
infected with melancholy
that push the past deeper into ruins.'

—the old houses sold, the Village
demolished. To dust.

You ask: 'Why did you leave?'
I answer: 'There is nothing left
to remind me to remember.
After the bricks fell and shattered
the villagers became anxious.'

You reply: 'Trepidation is God's
offering. Listen! There's no rush
to reach the future' — a turnpike
of unraveled lives, sun-bleached ghosts,
pale, tired.

All night long moths fly into the light,
into the stars, the flames. The wind stirs
their powdery ashes.
Body against body,

there is deep silence between us.
The waves break. The future rolls in,
disconnects the past.
The sea star falls from your hand.
Make a wish.

Understand

We are in flux
leaving time behind
and occupy ourselves
with nothing really

Perhaps it is time to begin over
to step away from our delusions
to lie entirely still

Tonight I drank this wine
it curses my blood

and my heart pulses
like a lonely dummy in a dark room
Tonight I want darkness to break silence
to tell me everything

I listen

listen

I have grievances that are voiceless
What is the point

I have come to love the silence the darkness
the end
and if these words appear out of confusion
then they are of understanding also

I push them out and let them live
longer than my own life

Hypnotize The Beast

I have seen the way a tongue
can slip out of its cage of teeth
and with insolent poison
and other toxic deliveries
can bite the self-confidence
of another

Its head snaps at the air
a malicious serpent
boneless and brutal
legless and swift
I have seen the way it thickens
with anger
boils in its own slush
wields saliva like viscous whips
generating a temper that spews
hot oil voodoo and spears

And like any other forceful beast
the modus operandi is
to feed it kindness
to make it drowsy on understanding
to cozy up to its moral conscience
to stroke its disagreeable condition
and bring it down to a whisper
and while it is panting and gasping
you slowly
shepherd it back into its cage of teeth
and give it a drink of cold water

That one is important
the cold water

We Are Only Sleeping

They began like storms, the tribal wars
of the world: the agitated colors of nations,
the bloodstained warriors, part good, part evil.
A great fright has crippled human love.

To spend whole days, whole years,
away from yourself, away from
your life, to live inside the will
of others, wedged in between
death and death as if living
without breathing, a legion

of hot lead, like charging horns,
coming from all directions,
hitting the flesh with iron fists:
the white crack of bones uprooted
out of the body

causing countless deaths by divisions
of boarders, by the odious gods
of faith: the opaque glass of hate is
a heavy pain.

We must hold tightly to the harmony
that is left, to bring the tribes together,
smoke swirling from peace pipes,
the flags of nations bleached
to the white cloths of surrender,
words of love in the cockpits of our mouths,
dive bombing, softly dive bombing,

the oil fields shut down, dead,
the great wind turbines humming,
solar panels sizzling.

Maybe a flock of arms in the flight of embracing,
maybe this is what's needed to refresh
our human need, to infuse bright energy
into our suppressed tranquility.

Some god

It would take a miracle
to undo ourselves,
a miracle, not a god,
to transcend the agitation
the dysfunction / the blathering
of sightless faith

Humanity needs something else
Maybe a mouthful of Belladonna
to scatter its nightshade
throughout our coursing blood
to still the wildness of our nerves
to drown our lungs in dried purple leaves
to drop us like shipwrecks laid out along
the floor of the sea
ghosts lifting through the mirage
of rescue lights: No Survivors

The ripened fruit is plentiful
in the orchard of wisdom
and still
most of humanity is like
a bell without a clapper
sort of pointless and dumb
or like an old wet sponge
swollen and dense
/ only / not with water but / with ignorance

And if some god were
to wring us out
and try to remake us
the water would be so russet
so murky and toxic
that some god would say:
'Oops'
and walk away / after tossing the sponge into
some hell

Then some god
would hide his own failure somewhere
deeply in the sky
infected water dripping from his hands
and his dark eyes / themselves / filled with
human turmoil

Nocturne in d-flat minor

In the same way breezeless trees are still
I ask for nothing
only to be.
Today is another demand,
the deep churning of time that quickens
the dust,
that which falls silently into the hole
till nothing is left
but the final sleep of exhausted flowers.
If I could translate this,
this thin string of old light,
it would be the loneliness
of a single shoe left behind.
If I could wake up and forget your absence
this empty heart would be less heavy.
I dare say nothing. Nothing.
Only I have spoken a few words too many.

Across a blue smear
wind-scattered clouds break apart.
They say nothing,
not even thank you
to the kindhearted wind
for its long body touches
each cloud's demise.

The wind is blind, so it only touches
still, it is possible to leave
to break apart
to enter the hole without feeling
to feel nothing
for what we leave behind.

Captivity

Today in the great wind
leaves fly
like quick flocks of red and yellow
and where autumn plasters its fresh ice
shadows are dense fabrics
that hang on blunt hooks
of walls and streets

Today there is no longer enough room
for the sun to heat up
but always enough puddles for the ice to swell

Today I can see the years-after
with their old scars
where age carries its face like
a worn out word calling ahead of itself
calling in between the disbelief
and the concern over
one eye then two going blind

Today makes no difference
because everything is getting smaller
and sees only the light
that it needs to see
maybe the light rising
or the light setting
or maybe it sees from a third eye
the one that has been the devoted witness
all along

and for those people
in the captivity of prayers
maybe they know more than I and maybe
their hands in prayer
hold all of the directions for the wind to blow
or maybe it is only one direction
that plays over and over again
that carries everything to the same place

Maybe the captivity of prayer is only
a hand gesture for hope
and maybe hope is nothing more than
the sound of a heart still beating

The Translator

A storm bends the small trees
nearly to the ground.
Only their will keeps them from
snapping. We stay alive
in the same way, resisting to stiffen,
to turn to ice or stone.

The wind is a glass shard ripping
the air, cutting the weak light.
Cruel. Unfeeling.
Some things are blown apart, blown away.

This dismal day is nearly hopeless as if blindness
at birth: a sightless soul plunged into a life
that is as unwanted as broken lamps.

Along the edge of town a train
charges the storm's vortex
and breaks through to the other side.
In dreams we see the other side,
an abstract to the same side
we are on. Both only halfway
to where we are going and

in between there is a message
that we can neither locate nor decipher
and we can only hope that it surfaces on time
with a proper translator.

Journey

If we close our eyes
and stand still
we can feel ourselves being pulled
into the future
and holding on tightly creates
an unwillingness to let go.

River reeds hold tightly to the mud
a steady drumming of current
against the silk of their slime
where glittery silverfish whistle
in the light, in the water's turnstile,
in the passageway.

The idea is to loosen our grip,
close our eyes, stand still,
to stop the mind's drag
by pushing when something pulls.
Push and pull, like insects loading
a nest: a swarm as strong as a blast,
the hum of dust waiting for the carrier,
the distance, the narrow aperture.

Everyone is an inhale, an exhale,
a natural death mask, an inward rage,
a sudden tear that loses grip
and is pulled into the tapered opening,
pulled the way an Exorcist pulls light
from the dark.

This is how we are buckled into
the passenger's seat:
riding shotgun into the future,
a finger on the trigger of apprehension.
This is how we come face-to-face
with the awakening, the remembering.

The Moon's Deep Wounds

When the soothing daylight
became absorbed
by the dim-colored distance
and the moon's beak
like a horde of splinters
hit with a thud against earth,
night fell with a rumble
that made no noise.

Then the abrupt moonlight
got caught in your dark hair
and the early evening air
untangled autumn's roots,
its twilight, its temple of leaves.

I watched you pull closer to yourself,
shaking like a thin spidery web.

You said: 'Maybe life is an invalid
or a guide gone astray and inside each
circle of breath there is a path of light
that winds around
and comes back to us … and … maybe …

(pause to shiver)

on the day that we are going to die the veil lifts
and we know exactly what it is that we need
and when we turn back to reach for it we fade away.'

Suddenly your gaze was that of a wolf,
calm and transfixed, unaware
of its divine ripeness and only aware
of its physical hunger.

You asked, rhetorically: 'If love is the master key
to the cosmic equation then why do lovers
become disjointed like worn out nets?'

Looking out over the wooded valley
where gray light feeds on the wilderness,
a jovial wind makes the leaves laugh and blur
and peel from the trees like orange embers
fleeing a fire.

In the dark stubble of the forest
the distance wavered, then disappeared.
The day was gone.

You continued: 'The bane of our existence
is cold sweat within the icy throes of sinister dreams.
There is too much drizzle, too much clutter.
Then nothing, nothing at all.'

We heard voices coming from along the river,
children's delicate voices, gentle laughter,
happiness the color of autumn, a crackling fire.
White smoke rose from the valley's black shroud, rose
like ghostly medicine over the moon's deep wounds

and the wind shifted to a steady chilled motion.
You shuddered in silence.
Overhead, the noisy geese made their escape
and every leaf was shaking.

Origin

I have come to find the origin
of death.
Heavens, written in fables, lost
in mistranslation and guarded
by idols. Infinity: living, dying,
the heritage of the spirit,
one part light,
one part dark.

I have come to unearth the origin
of the end:
we pass from belly to grave,
from cradle to cremation,
from nest to dust. The nakedness
of all: wood, feather, bone.

To explore the origin of death I find
a center that is
the law of the heart: a wet sail for the body,
the moisture of love beneath
rice paper skin that peels from its memory.

Birth, an ignition from a star,
an unfolding of nerves
that rises from its origin: a woman's body
breaks water. A shell offers its pearl.

These gestures, offering and taking,
crowd between creation
and destruction: truth, myth,
the stinging birth slap. A wingless bird
leaves the nest. The Equinox,
the Solstice, each
the origin of the other.

Urgency

Buried beneath the roots
the nether-region is a river
of dust, glass shards,
seashell pieces, aged minerals.

I hold a handful of soil
and hear the dead, like cattle
herded together. They walk
barefoot through the dust.

Having forgotten the lilt
of their voices, I place my ear
to the earth, to the past, my heart
pounds like a wet mallet.

Death stands before us, behind us,
collecting the flying embers
of each life and the days become
shut down by spent time.

At the end of every season
is an urgency: the harvesting
of old age, the dehydration of gods,
miracles, twilight.

Dust

What we think about
is our motion
almost never our stillness
What we dig into
is our past
almost never our future
We make tunnels
through the fallout
through the stretch
of remains that lie
from there to here
We climb our tree
and rummage through
our ancestors
searching for a likeness

In a rush of motion
we unearth
unfamiliar roots
locks of hair
faded photographs
bundles of letters
and dried roses pressed
in between tattered pages
of secret love journals

We almost never think about
the future that it all comes to
when the dust
falling from our hands
is a weightless net cast over
the attic floor
The burden of years
having amassed their toll
their detachments their indifferences

Spring, A Birthing Womb

Spring's leaves harmonize with the sun's warm nuance,
a sweetness of lilacs, daffodils, milk-light calla lilies.

A seasonal meditation: a moth cocoons
near a thousand orange blossoms.

Hands are the breezes, the essence of touch,
you hold your palm out and trace
the shadow of a honeybee whose lineage
is the garden's bounty.

You say: 'Beneath our skin is the run
of a red river. If we listen to its reason
then the salt of body, sea and earth
will form as one essential current.'

I love the way that you visualize
as the breeze visualizes: a voyager
whose plans are unique. You caress
the shadow in your hand and whisper
a noun: 'Body'

You say: 'There is light beneath shadows
an open aperture, an impulse to appear:
Confident. Faithful. Eternal. Listen!
Connect the shadows with their native ink,
let them consume the light's darkness,
to know the architecture of their existence.'

I hold out my palm and feel the red river
running. I wait for a shadow to appear,
wait for its nakedness to lie quietly in my hand.

You continue: 'The wings of bees are verbs
irrigating the air. Their inheritance is the sugary
pollen that drifts like barefoot dust, like dry
water songs, like a flower's origin. Comfort
the shadow. It is your identity. The body
of awakening.'

Weightlessly, as if falling from the sky,
a shadow lands in my palm, dips into
the red river and drinks my human honey.
The palm of my hand: a barren valley,
a salt block, a warm hearth.

When my eyes open I see you
on the far shore of the bed, sheltered
by waves of yellow floral sheets.
The earth has turned so that the sun ignites
the orange tree. Blue skin of sky, crisp
like pressed paper.

I rise and look out at the garden.
A tapestry of spring is a birthing womb
and everywhere newborn shadows feed
from the light and, like a moth's cocoon,
I sit in meditation. My body, like huge hands
in prayer, gives birth to a shadow.

Together, we feed from the light.

Wildcat Canyon

Sitting at the edge of the canyon,
orange sunset displays a dazzling radiance.
Shadows drop their ink as if smudged words
on dry pages.

Sitting close to you
I feel your unrelenting loneliness
while the canyon flexes its golden tone
over the blue oak and summer lupine.
It moves across the air to the other side.

You say: 'If we had wings there would be
a rhythm understood as hovering, first,
only to fly along the horizon's thin string. There,
human ignorance would find its blissful balance,
would find the truthful verses excluded at birth.'

As the light steadily recedes, the rugged
expanse of the canyon resembles
a thirsty moon's dehydrated craters.
A coyote's wild philosophy echoes
against the vast stretch of exposed inner earth.
Turkey vultures drift and float
like expressive dark capes. Now the sun
squishes its hot cherry, the sky spills red.

You say: 'A supreme form, a star's energy generates
its own bliss. A phosphorescent being-absolute,
unmatched, and measured by its dominant flame
and most people stare in confusion asking asinine questions:
Was there a beginning? Is there an ending?'

The evening's warm air, lightly scented with seawater,
drifts in from the nearby bay. Behind us
July's moon begins its rise as if a streak of light
from a door left ajar. I take your hand in mine.
Your eyes close and you say:

'The sun's energy tempers our marrow,
spikes our nerves and converts its heat
into dreams, thoughts and speech
that has become more agitation than pleasure.
Loneliness: a flame that dies inside of us.
Haunting pain: stillborn dreams left behind.'

Unsure if my presence is a consolation
or a bizarre symbol for your chronic lonesomeness,
I remain silent. Your hand slips from mine.
A mountain lion's cry peals like a wicked bell.
Nervously, blacktail deer move into thorny thickets,
the night drops its ink-sac and in their hysteria
cicadas begin to shriek.

You stand up as if needing to do something.
Night's arrival is a mirror that reflects your restless shape
and the presence of your hopelessness accumulates
and defines the weight of your emptiness.
I stand up and in silence we walk back to the truck.
Wanting. Wanting nothing. Wanting everything. Waiting.
Waiting for nothing. Waiting for everything.

When You Drown You Float

At the City's edge a steel factory
releases its gung-ho scream
The air shivers in damp skin
shakes and ripples
A gust of wind planes
over a seamless hold of dust
that smothers thirsty foliage
Diminished light is uncaring
All of this which seems to never
fade is more important than
the oblivion where everything
throws its old milk
In the middle of life one can see
both start and finish and how
the body shrinks away from the soul
Nothing is easier than the body's
skeleton handing the soul over
to a new cycle of contradictions
But today I walk along the edge
and see orange swabs
of youthful poppies feeding on
parched earth along side
dry notes from insects that
may or may not be cryptograms
If only I could translate this network
of dusty lines Maybe if I put my eyes
to the ground or let my body sink
into earth just a little maybe
this effort will be an expression
of my clueless existence
of my yearning to let go
to sit inside my soul and look out
like a genie, waiting.

Appearance

Fog wraps the city in its own grudge,
drags east to dampen the suburbs.
Late noon light, a dark soul against
the steady lick of traffic over August asphalt.

Now the fog drops like a wet handkerchief
then lifts like a gray bird and stretches
its appearance.

What if, for example, we could stretch
our appearance and convince others
that we are not what we used to be?
Lets say like a bud that has opened
or a scatter of dust that lifts
from the ground, crosses the wind
and dips into a puddle. Dissolves.

If appearance is the required shine
that we buff out in the morning then
it is also the heavy grime that we drag
behind us at day's end, stepping out
of the commute line like a fake coin
ejected from a slot machine.

Now the air is soaked in muscle-bound
moisture as if a sponge left behind
at a water hole and the appearance of the day
has so severely shifted that a trail of wind
is a wet shirt flapping on a line and snapping
my face. This day's hopes have fallen

so far behind that I can see it in the aching
facial lines of staggering office workers.
I see it in the tight stitch of cars jammed
at the tollgate. I see it through the train's
windows, the cattle cars of suburbia, whose
appearance forms an icy, metallic smear,
the riders, frozen shoulder to shoulder, harassed
by the flickering strike of fluorescent venom.

Even the city's appearance has changed
by the liquid pewter the fog has poured
over it: appearance then may be an overly
explosive flash in a whitewashed photograph
that is as useless as a sun without light.

Now the fog is something of a wet blizzard
with the sun's electric lines crackling
somewhere behind it. Summer's appearance
vacated by a misted, white chill.

Rattle

The tan ropes are rattlesnakes
that tie and untie themselves,
clumps of spines untangled
from earth, loops and S's
curling like damaged ribs.

My body is a tight cage that
the snakes move away from.
My hands: closed canyons,
manzanita, sage, moon-dew
marked by footprints.

I watch you pick one up, feeling
distress from its rattle cut into
my nerves. Heat from its mouth
hisses like splintered glass.
You hand it to me,

it crawls through my fingers:
skinny road-lines on a map
charting the back fields
that lead to the foothills. Red dust
flames in the air. Dry rain falls.

A voice says: 'It is a conspiracy.
This is how they do it: They shed
their skin to be unrecognized
in the future. Their shed skins
are thoughts with blank memories.'

The voice continues: 'Be cautious
of the young ones. They will charm you
with their bodily curves then secretly
overthrow you, defame you
and trouble your future.'

I stand here in the red foothills
and can see the snakes have no empathy.
Like a shot, something burns my ears
and burns my hand: a hot pistol. Suddenly,
dawn sun-paints my bedroom.

I lie silently still listening to my mind's
unfinished opinions. The insides of my thighs,
fiery like a venomous bite, the sheets cast off
like shed skin and my thoughts flame and burn
like morning's dry mouth.

Lead and Salt

So often I come close to the crack point
then pull myself together
No concern for this wrecked world
all I can do is go into myself
conjure a hole
caste these feelings to the bottom
where the light is displaced
dries out
where dust scatters
like a shy apparition
and leaves the world behind

darkness of days

darkness of nights

darkness of lives

darkness of deaths

unseen void

severed air

darkness of death

There must be lead in my lungs
or a heavy sea that is all salt
I could list more complaints
but what is the use
because my weakness is for life
and not for a dying world
yet this weakness draws me closer

closer to death

Kleptomaniac

To swarm is to know the overthrow
the lose of honey
the bust that makes one run
How atypical one must be
to have nothing / to encounter
the dry crackle of isolation
like the dull mark of Buddha
in the grips of emptiness
a sharp buzz of silence
from one ear to the other
There must be rust
at the end of infinity
something that hollows out desire
or bruises it until it rots
How far is it / the destination
that pumps forward
the destination that drags life behind it?
The breakable heart pumps forward
like an oiled cog in motion
two hot beats in succession
the percussive thud of flaps
opening and closing
So many say they have nothing
nothing to do / nothing to wear
nothing to love

How atypical one must be
to have nothing / to encounter
the dull mark of Buddha
in the grip of emptiness
to be nothing more than
a kleptomaniac
shoplifting happiness from nothing

Yuba

Campfire blazes and wavers
like desert curtains at sunrise.
Orange skin beneath dry sky,
red blood knitted to blue veins.
A spread of smoke flutters, ripples
as if silk ascends, floats away.

At the river's edge, barefoot
in the wild mud, you are an egret,
a water song, a smooth rock, sensual
and meditative. Further out, light
and breeze are lively nerves against
the dark wooded shore, against
the weight of dusty boulders.

You say: 'The more that we indulge
in the river's gospels and hymns the less
we will question existence and the raw heat
between earth and stars, the very element
that we are, is clear truth, is pain and pleasure,
is remembering and forgetting.'

The fire hisses and spits as if a nest of lizards.
The river murmurs like a wondrous huge moth.
Dawn's light lifts higher to the valley's steeple,
to the tips of fir, lit like majestic candles.
Within my human cave, my human emptiness
I am anxious to believe you.

You say: 'Confusion is a whimper, a deep sigh
from a mountain lion's sleep. Life is breath
set on fire by no one that burns out with use.
Memories are lights along the journey
that become diffused lamps.'

I watch you step into the river,
the water casts its formation around
your thighs. You shiver: a featherless bird.
Your long, dark hair gestures the breeze
with a tribal poise that is the mythology,
the passage, the shadow severed from the body,
the breath that leaves no trace.

You say: 'The Spirit-Seed spreads its roots
throughout earth, unfurling from the sky,
falling from dead stars into the water.
Water resonates inside our bodies. It hems
the stardust into bones and nerve centers,
into voices, into living and dying.
Life is the bullet and death is the spent
cartridge so, upon reaching the expiration
date, why must we turn as pale and empty
as an abandoned chrysalis?'

Being that you are facing the Yuba
and speaking, I am not sure if this question
is for me. I remain silent and watch
sunlight drape like amber tapestry over
the edge of the forest and cross the water.
Trout become angels swimming. Reeds
are yellow guideposts. River snakes are
dark gray mountain roads on a wet map.
Somewhere the rapids are booming,
like furious storms, agitated, aggressive.

I place a log on the fire and watch it flame
into sunburn on its back. Above the Yuba
a golden eagle hovers then dives and lifts
a rainbow trout into the sky.

You remove your sheer dress and your seductive
nakedness disappears beneath cold water.
I count the seconds as if a dream has left you
unfinished, as if each air bubble is a silent scream
as if I have woken up alone with nothing,
with nothing at all.

Worthy

I have come to where Autumn
smears its blush
to where the days are burnt seconds
that pass like short candles

An old ghost loiters with icy hands
and ponderous clouds wait
to secure rain to the empty streets
as if the rain will stay forever
but nothing will last
even the wind has turned older
less skillful and is tired from singing
Some days it lies broken like a cracked flute

We are sinking into earth
the roots of termination grow into our feet
the harvest of the dead
written on calendar days
and the noiseless part of the end
consigns memories to the past

The final stillness will lead us

I do not know the words
to explain this
My ignorance is full and my explanation
would not matter

The future comes to be left behind
the sun rises to bleed at day's end

and none of this
is worthy of too much regard
even as we make up reasons
to say that it is

Time Is Nothing When It Is Dark

As if the windows are stained black
and always with a tang of sleeplessness
Two AM shapes its moonless light
and doles out restlessness.

Time is nothing when it is dark, nothing more
than a latched gate to a narrow path where
he feels contained and smaller. Everything
is uncaring and passes by like flimsy smoke
or is unkind like an old mirror held in his hand.

The sound of a decayed car grows insistently:
rattling, groaning, creaking. Headlights cast
their illusions. He listens: voices drop to the road
as if severed from mouths. Abandoned phrases
remain in their drama. A loose windowpane vibrates
from the engine's trembling. Then silence.

He reads a book to withdraw from the hour.
It, too, is old in his hands: the wet pulp of trees
skinned alive, a tapestry of leaves left thirsty
and dying on the forest floor. He turns the pages
as if each one is a patch of life withered to illness
in a musty mill. Still, the hours do nothing more
than exist.

He looks out of the window and sees faint stars
fluttering as if wind-blown tissues snagged by barbs.
His eyes climb the sky. His body does not follow.
Everything is still as in still waiting.

He watches the darkness crowd the streets
crowd in between the houses, crowd the trees
crowd the plain face of the insensate streetlamp
whose light is frail and partially impotent, watches
where it vanishes in the shadows. He leans
against the wall, a carcass of no faith.
His thoughts have gone deaf and dumb.

The book falls from his hand as if a leaf from a tree
skinned alive. The hour bumps up to Three AM.
The pane's thin glass vibrates again. Another car
moves dumbly down the road with the vacant expression
of an insomniac's face.

Invisible

I could not sleep
imagining it must be raining
There is darkness inside these clouds

I have come to know this feeling
this obscured emptiness
All night there is nothing
but my breathing
and there is a nebulous death
that happens between breaths

The sky bends around me
touches the trees
and knifes its way between the branches

I stand in the cold air
as a child stands in winter's whisper
snow angels freshly painted
and pinned to the ground

It seems that there is still
something
that I need to say
to support this melancholy
to bear witness to the sorrow
the world owns
Could this darkness be a god
that takes me to the other side
where what is left is
invisible
Tonight the moon is unseen
by its own absence

How many more thoughts
must I make
to understand the world
to understand the joy of some
the grief of others

Halos and Harps

He walks along the dry day

Winter

no rain has streamed

Under a solar flood

his shadow appears disconnected

like a sketch of a body

that is not his

The shadow may be death

coming

out of the ground

to breathe his air his life

He looks up and sees

the other side of the sky

it is dark

and nothing like the fables tell

nothing of light or harps

or angels

and everyone there is homesick

and all of the halos that he made

as a child

have been shattered

Sometimes Belief Needs A Telescope

To travel the distance
we must lighten ourselves
by throwing off the coverings:
the disquiet, distractions, discontent
the constant motion and sound.
To believe that we are real is not
the intention of I AM, nor is it real,
this emptiness from looking into mirrors.
To travel the distance
we must give everything
to the unknown purity
which is calculated
by the invisible: detachment
is a thought set free
or physical contortions while the body
transforms to melodious stillness.
Death is weightless because
it lives in a future that does not exist.
To love is to know everything
within the juxtaposition of knowing nothing.
To travel the distance we must
shred all words that sound like doubt
we must make ourselves buoyant
by unloading the pain, the damage,
the fallout, by turning our lead into gold
our tears into crystals
our thoughts into prisms.

A Far-Flung Future

You say: 'Every time we close our eyes
to blink and open them again
we are in the future and the past
is a windblown paper bag.'

Your eyelids are clear canopies
to a cove's opening marked by light
and dark, and the future is a scientist
collecting memory specimens.

I examine your theory like a traveler
checking their luggage. I scroll my thoughts
to see if this is a dream or another anticipation
to the moment before we touch.

In this dream: Morning is the blood
that warms us in a desert of rusted trucks.
Earth feeds from their radiators
and drinks the syrupy brown water.

You continue: 'If we do not blink
the future never happens, never
lays out its blueprint, except, our eyes
will become as waterless as drought.'
I hand you a cactus flower and hope
for a meaningful conversation.
In this dream: Our tongues become erasers.
When our lips touch to kiss
everything disappears.

This is where I wake up: my body
at the edge of flames. Hand-painted
minerals burn on a sill near a cracked pane.
Leaves drop like skulls from unraveled skin.

I don't know how to interpret dreams
and when I woke up my dry tongue
was flailing like a grounded finch
and the white ceiling,

a flock of snow geese smeared across the sky
and the future is somewhere without us:
everyone blinking, blinking.

The Sound Of Bones

Time has cut lines
into my face
An arc of light fires its torch
burns the lines into dry rivers

I shake my head
dust falls into my mouth

Tomorrow is only a handful of breath
that will cling to my lungs

I do not want to joke with or misjudge death
because like the shadow of an exhale
I am not really here

Suddenly and all at once
I breathe in again
and the sound of my bones
singing

wakes me

A Dream Held In A Mouth

Feel:

when spirit is felt there is

purity. pure.

from the inside.

See:

decay is purity

death a sunset

a painted flame.

Grief:

a shadow removed

breath becomes ether.

A dream held in a mouth

eyes closed

becomes a passageway

that calls back

that calls forward

that crawls out.

Awake.

Observation, Recollection

Full Life In The Day Of A Poet

The Poet Writes:

Dawn. The sun's big display creates its fortune.
The Poet rises in a beam. Small birds chirp
near the Poet's smile. The day's marvelous
reality. A phenomenon. Should the Poet
doubt reality when it lives in his senses?

The Poet Writes:

Noon. A sudden change in the hour's hand,
light floats its bright balloon. The birds insist,
more songs. The afternoon's various glitters
are thrown into the air. The Poet's mind,
a warm breeze flows.

The Poet Writes:

Night. A crimson lavender sky
ushers the darkness. Nighttime's stillness
spills from creation's hands. The Poet
is silent. Memories burn his nerves.
Like an octopus, his hand clutches a pencil.
Like fine hairs, splintered graphite falls to the paper.

The Poet Writes …

Naked Cry

I awoke in April
light
morning
color of snow and leaves

an angel
pulled from sky to earth
ether to breath
cloud to gift
a sprout
from human seeds

First without sound
nobody knew me
my voice
fixed firmly inside
and in spanking fresh skin
I waited to be heard

It was late morning
there was cold there was hunger
my wings were gone
and a voice called out
my new name and
another voice called my name

quickly my lungs unglued
and I cried
my naked cry

Teachers

Morning's teachers come from where
light inks its ribbon
and types descriptions of the day

Because the air is still
it is a warm page
of fast verbs, short flights
birdsong crescendo

The sun breaks

Late August dawn consumed
like sand tossed into a canyon
the damp earth begins to dry

In the houses I imagine lovers
as wet paint rising from the canvas
to greet the painter's face
to know the goodness in his smile

Oak branches reaching up
seek the hands that created them
and there is a lesson here, a lesson in
how pure a moment can be
Looming autumn presses yellow lines
into green leaves and calls out to the rain
Assemble!   Assemble!

The last of the blackberries, withered
under dust

Raven

Outside my window on a leafless branch
and covered in lingering moonlight
a raven
with its craggy croak
was measured against the red sunrise
that had splayed the east
in prophecy

Red sky in morning
sailors take warning

The raven was close enough
that I could see leftover stars
reflected in its circular eyes
and the watery moonlight
slid off of its smooth body

The raven's low croak was at times
like dry thistle
prickly throaty and territorial
and at other times a dusty antique song
or black seeds that sprout thorny weeds

Having placed the sound of its business
in my ears
the raven was restless edgy
fluttering and preening
or cocking its head
observing me with one eye then the other

I smiled and tapped against the pane
and like a thrilling illusionist
the raven vanished

Sweeping Heaven

The bent-over old man knows
You can tell by the winter in his eyes
and how he rakes the leaves
slowly

Sadness detaches him from conversation
he sees no value in words
he is tired of life
and misses his wife
Slowly he rakes the leaves

His son lives faraway
seldom comes around
and when he does he is anxious
to get home to wife and child
and slowly
the old man rakes

In autumn's chill
the old man is an empty self of a past
that had affectionate pleasures
and attention to necessities
now slowly he rakes the leaves
like an angel sweeping heaven

He is preparing

Harbor Scene

Along the sandy floor of the beach
this empty place
now deep into the season
The dragging hiss of foamy water
joins the cold dust of autumn
a steady wind sweeps
the footprints of summer

The ocean stirs like a restless flight
of anxious gulls and empties
the wings of its waves
into a dry nest upon the rocks
A spirited flock of sandpipers
peck for nutrients
in the sheer glaze of water
that continually crawls back to the sea

The harbor's breath is a sauté
of fish, salt, driftwood, ocean greens
and the lofty whitewashed lighthouse
plays its instrument for the fog
and blinks its glassy eye
at the season's long evenings

The wet-netted voices of fishermen
tying down lines and hosing off decks
grow as thin as frost in this chilled air
amongst the baritone barks of sea lions
groping over one another for a mouthful
of the day's haul

Far off, tracking the horizon, a freighter
holds steadily to the slight line drawn
between sea and sky
From its stack a gray-black smoke blows
heavy and dense
like a nasal sickness blows its nose

The harbor is crammed with sailboats
deserted and sail-less, being rocked to sleep
by churning water and a retarded lullaby
from the wind chime clanking
of rigging hardware against masts

Perched on the pier's thick wooden rail
two brown pelicans
bundled in the dim coat of early evening
With eyelids closed the day's catch
marinates in their warm stomachs
as night's full-length begins to tuck itself
beneath the fog

Leisurely walking the pier and freshly packaged
in fall fashion
a young couple presses into each other's warmth
the way noon shadows press into hot adobe walls
as the imposing air from autumn's icy saturation delivers
a tight aching emptiness seldom known by lovers

Over time the night comes to a tranquil pause
The fishermen are gone the sea lions are quiet
the wind has evolved to a soft-knitted breeze
and the rocking sailboats have settled down
to a subtle sway

Rain #2

As if the sky were an aspergillum
this autumn rain spreads
like a sprinkled blessing

Rapidly the daylight turns dim
with a gray as complete
as a thin ghost
and I can hear the water drip
like unhurried secretion from each leaf

The gray spreads as if dust in a windy
Film Noir
and gnaws on the leftover pale
August flowers

Perhaps this too is heaven:
autumn's decay, abandoned branches,
the lingering fragile terracotta yarrow
all of it held captive, bitten and bruised

near stones deepening their footings
with raindrops deepening earth's wrinkles

Now sorrow shakes its feelings

rattles its silence

crosses its heart

and hands me a poem

City Portrait

The jangle from church bells

unnerves the trees

At the edge of the hills

nighttime thins its residue

as light splatters and splays

another sunrise

and the world shoots forward

into the passing lane

Men's and women's

accelerated footsteps

are flames against

the punch of the hour

The buses and trains chime and whistle

doors close heads nod

as the sun pushes the sky open

and the Bay's water goes blind

like a dazzled eye

Circle

At the circle the fountain bubbles
and the melody the spouting water croons
slips

into the heads of clouds
or hums
as it splashes on the grass

One by one the water drops
the dust flies
and the traffic moves slowly
in circles
round and round

The water sounds like
a mute wooden bell when
its laziness sits there
in the basin
waiting

In a streak of magic
a woman tosses a penny
and the copper glow
is a footstep
hitting the water

and the light nurses the ripples
and over there a child sings
louder than a mockingbird

(The 1911 Marin Circle fountain, North Berkeley, California)

Scenes From Cedar Park

There is an old face
sitting on a bench
wind presses against the face
reverberation from cars resonates and drifts
Under the fog
the shadows have perished
A cyclist flashes along the path
at the same time a raven
sustains its low flight
The old face nods off
and fallen eyelids of thin balsawood
board out the light
the face tilts sideways then slumps

A young mother's hand
shapes around her toddler's head
the child thinks it is reading a book
the pages are upside down
no one listens to the child's voice
as each word is a weightless tone
but the child is easily amused
The mother looks at the old face
the face holds its wrinkles
and the young mother holds her child closer
as if the old face is a mirror
showing her something

The Bird Flew Off

Now the hours drag and rust.
Colors drain their complexions.
I dare not move in dismay of the emptiness.

There is nothing left but sleep: the soft bells
sigh at the hand that holds the lifeless clapper.
Breath passes unnoticed.

In the middle of the night your wet lashes
spilled over the mirror. You collected
your sorrow, tears spoke. Your loneliness
stumbled and left.

Nighttime knocks harder against the forgotten,
rain slaps the panes. My eyes blur then focus
like a weathercock in the direction of your absence:

murky stillness, dark chill, dejected bare feet
crossed cold wooden floors,
the empty rectangle of the open door.

After the wind blew there was nothing
but a strand of your black hair
dangling nakedly. Maybe your scent
like a faint bird in flight.

A Trumpet Blows The Blues

It begins in thought
and sounds like static from a tube radio
your voice that lives inside
speaking
as if it were real

Restless is my mind
in the fracture of this night
the chilled breeze
like hovering mosquitoes
thin and sure of themselves

I am here
beneath the rise of your voice
tangled in unease
in the middle of self
a retarded star that succumbs
to a snuffer

the smoke rises
into the breeze
trembles then drifts
like a trumpet blowing the blues

Tonight the cold light of your eyes

haunts me

memories cut my heart

Tonight I am the half note

that can not sing

that can not make it

to the top of the scale

Corrosion

There is rust inside this dream.
What is known, what is not.
It is morning now, flat light
through cracks. Somehow
your lips, your hair, the wet tangle
crosses time
movement unfolds

the middle of summer

fog arrives again.

Your face, your open eyes
thrive in memory, mythology.

The mind's ledger, too many entries
too many readers.
A familiar gloom rises, passes
and leaves its corrosion.

I am caught again.

The sky is black, gray, white.
This is how morning sounds: the crows
speak my language. In dull light
I am faceless. A woman's red jacket
is a burning body.

The breeze blows its flute, two notes.
A small green banner applauds then again
quietly sleeps.

What is here is all there is, a piece of this world
this piece that is too heavy to lift
too corroded to carry forward.

I lift this dream anyway and try to carry it further
before the gods wake up
and tell me it is not mine.

Morning's Mirror

In morning's mirror
the unforgiving light
tortures his face
and digs into the trenches
Caught in the reflection
his exhausted expression
from uneasy dreams
is not amusing
and still there are parts of his mind
that are entertained

From what he can see
wrinkles are the laughing mouths
of death
the dried-lipped smiles of an aged carcass
maybe dead leaves in late autumn's garden

Wake up!
A splash of icy water, then two,
then three: Wake Up! The world is alive
and there is more to be done while waiting
for the lines to connect.

Departures: 1958-1964

There was so much death
that I thought
death was the only way to live
One after the other
they walked out of their bodies
and into the invisible
The faces of the living
paralyzed with grief
and how heartlessly the dark sky fell
on each fresh grave
as earth pulled them in
pulled them out of sight
and the rigid ache of gravestones
like tightly packed arthritic pain

Between these years there were
several departures
and so many times the clouds bit down
with an overly mournful rain
and there was nothing to feel
but a shiver of sky
gripped by the metallic air
and all of the rain was enough
even for the dead

Hymn

I can only think of what is:
cold thunder of grief
moan of disbelief
dust to dust
quiet as cloud to cloud

I'll sing a hymn
only to hug your heart
only to calm the nights
and the waves of lakes
pooling inside your eyes:

cupped in your hands
the sound from each drop resonates
loneliness

Sing ... sing a hymn with me
even if voiceless
let the silence heal the emptiness
until you are full
until the clouds pass
until your hands no longer drown
beneath the lake

(for Heather M. Browne)

Eulogy For Roses

A wrinkled day
red roses faded blush
Pretty dead flowers
sink into earth
wrought with sighs
till nothing beckons

There is a burn
in each nerve there is a burn

Lets wish this day goodbye
this day good luck
this day raised by sun
lowered by moon

This day petals fell
tumbled then shriveled
till motion lost hope
and folded
like an empty hand

Ghost

A lifeless body of newsprint
is given soul
by a night-wind's updraft
a single abandoned wing
black and white feathers

Moonlight, streetlight,
houselights

a lit joint, a long drag

Exhale

Smoke expelled from my mouth
becomes the skin of a ghost or swirling
white cursive over black vellum

The ash floats to the ground
radiates in the moonlight
a dry river covered in snow

Memories are pulled along
like an old red wagon
the rusted axles of life
I drag again and the ghost reappears
clings to the edge of my lips
Releases Floats

The sacredness of this mundane moment
between myself
and this nocturnal crevice
The cleverness of gravity
pulling the ash to the ground

and me in my nightly structure
of solitaire, all cards played out
A lexicon of harlequin thoughts
like fireworks in my head

I drag again only to have
the recurring ghost as company

Going Coastal

My heart is bound to the coast
to the cliffs that have mastered
the edge, to the sea that extends
its directions, to the sand that sails
the wind, to the waves that fold
like skin

I depend on the journey of seabirds
on the lighthouses like bleached stars,
on the horizon's concise line, on the
sunset's poised flames, on the current
that holds its stare, on the current
that drags jellyfish, on the current
that radiates pull

I see passing ships as small fuses
that bind sky and water, the sky's
background that holds the window
open, the sky's blue, the sky's gray
the storms that etch into stones
the storms that hem sea and sky
into curtains

I depend on the coast with its driftwood
laid out like edgy scars
its driftwood that rises like bones
its driftwood that sleeps like a smile
and the fog that nods off like a dull lamp
the fog that sits like a wet dog

My heart is bound to the sun's glare
that sets the sea reflecting like
a large mirror, that sets the sea
glistening without hesitation
glistening like a steady boulevard
like sparkling electricity in the middle
of nowhere

And the dunes along the sea
shanties of sand or soft cushions
as if overly stuffed chairs
magnificent and cozy

Sundown

In rotation, the crusted earth
Winter solstice
guides my journey
I feel myself like wind
casting the sea

The old squabbles of seagulls
parched against the late sun

Horizon: a thread of sea and sky
Prone Calm Level

Now the crusted earth
is an orange weave
twisted with cypress
and needled with drift

How simply the last blaze floats
bobs, releases
then dives under the watery blue
like a vessel
for the sun's blinding resin

Exposed and somber
darkness drops
then quickly rises

Nocturne

Timeless:
the surf's ageless boom hushes the sunset
and the water drags a bluesy nocturne
under the breakers

The night-sky chars the dim light
and the full moon
expands low above the small harbor
like a slow lump of yeast rising
and little by little
carries its caldron of embezzled light
into the sky's black mud

Diminished
the sharp light turns flat

Twelfth Installation

December's moon

circular ivory skull

alabaster bone

It hangs as a porcelain prize

on a plate hook

I think of a dark hole

that it may fill

or the antique lamp that it may be

or the eye of a lighthouse

far from shipwrecks at sea

Its glow wraps the sky

in stunning circles

of illumination

weightless and downy

Maybe it is a sheet of round white paper

glued to a black stone

or maybe the stamp of an artist

on a finished installation

In The Body Of A Daydream

Primary light:

the ocean is anointed

with spilt moon oil

Sacrifice: lucid breakers

burdened

by the perfection of salt

The sky's consciousness

does not judge

Winter brings its old eyes

thinly lacquered

with the lifting sun's lazy glaze

To stand close

to the back and forth scroll

of waves: opening, closing

Something sinks deeper

beyond flesh

Something resonates

repeats

from blood to bone

nerves to marrow

Rejuvenation. Soul

calls out, as human, as divinity

Soul answers:

From inside out we resurrect

Embrace

Against the craggy cliffs

I press into the landscape

The chords of the ocean

played from my lungs

This mild eve: a chilled palm

moves over my eyes. The clouds

gather their bundles. Motion:

the magic of breeze.

I am lulled by a thin streak of blue

by the blur of crested waves

by the dark plumage of cormorants

I have built my feet into the sand

and watch myself dream

to the bottom of the sea:

a fathomless consciousness

swabs my spirit, a tug of current

pulls me along

Embrace. I believe in my dream

and drift. My body

a salt-bright sea blossom

a wave stilled by its own death

a circle of light

upward

jingling the sky

Mountains

In the distance
the silence mountains make
I listen: sky
is mirth, gesture, glitter
Dreamy wind: Trees
flute voices Whirling
a feathered moon
raises a crystal beak
then floats its contagious body
over the rim and cloaks
the summit in full-length
white wings Listen
to the silence
mountains make
rising above the valley
and the stars
hot against the canvas
each one inflamed like Van Gogh's
discarded ear. Starry night
Feathery moon Alabaster peaks

The Willowed Landscape

Within these words
is the deep sleep of willow wood
where moon-sap
trails into spring
A crystal clear breeze
unties then reties the leaves
and consumes wine-green
from April's cup

The sky's handsome blue head
is in a trance
perched upon bright light
and birds are floating ornaments
strung together

The sun blares like a highlighter marking
the willowed landscape lemon yellow
Dandelions spin their miniature cotton
A warm taffy breeze then again
stillness

Enchanted

In sheer fog
the Santa Lucia's wear a thin
silvery gauze
as if earth's body has transformed
only to guide me beneath
the morning's moon

Spread across the meadow
a herd of dappled light
like sheep set out to graze

Lifted by this chilled wind
a tired yellow leaf rises and flutters
as if a leftover pulse from autumn's
old vein

and I am enchanted
by the features of mist
mountains
leaf and light
and the discourse of crows
above the stillness of sheep

silence

a faded April moon

Solo Flight

In this valley of earth
the wind
comes with the same gift
the same solitary wind
that carries faith
without speaking

with the same sightless purity
that sees everything
as it is
that causes the same quiver of branches
that have pulled their skins
out of soil and rocks

The wind's long horn blows
into this valley's earthen jug
and applies its wisdom
as thin as
this silver hair that holds the heat
to my bones

this wisdom that assembles
and stirs above me watching
and me standing
below
in this valley as cold as heaven
where there has always been
and even now a river's
unsaid oath
where birds drop feathers
where birds balance the wind
even in sleep

even when nothing moves
even when knowing that
each feather dropped
can fly

alone

each one
gifted with the wind's wisdom

Gardener

My hands are the hands
of a gardener
fresh with soil, sunlight, and rain
with breath of flowers
and kisses of moisture
I sprinkle seeds over the earth
like a holy man sprinkles sacred water
The soil: grateful for my blessing
The birds: grateful for this small fare
I chant incantations and listen
for the growth of roots
for the rustle of sprouts
pastel green and tender, spiritual
and uplifting
I rain dance and praise the sky
hold my hands to the air
forming a small bowl
for the rain to fill
to be the stimulus, the birthmother
the liquid that makes
the garden whole
I ask the sun for waves
of light, the breeze
for strength and circulation
the fertilizer for sparkling minerals
that infuse the roots, stems and fruit
with vitality
On my knees I dig
with bare hands into the soil:
my hands like intimate dancers
lead the busy prolific weeds
to another existence, to their rebirth
My hands are the hands
of a gardener
fresh with soil, sunlight and rain

Queen

The way the bees pull apart the Borage
pack their bags and fly off
I raise my head
and pluck the air with my lips
marvel at their weightlessness
at the way they stain the sky
when they swarm

Striking against the sun
their toy-yellow appearance
is a child's design that floats
from the bottom up
small stars of exquisite bitterness
a wood-fire of stingers
minute eyes of splintered black ice

They have invented a secret
the persuading of waterless pollen
into Royal Jelly
while the queen dominates
with her dangerous sex
the pure poison of ecstasy
spilling a violent sweetness

Sun

The certainty of always
sun
its limitless clamor

Under the sky it magnifies
blood-warmth, landscapes
the beauty of loneliness

Primal energy, unleashed
and realized
it built its temple, set its tempo
and most life is drawn to it
mixed by it, baked by it

Glory, praise, sun, circle of gold
deadly impurities, fury, irritation
inflamed brew

Glory, praise, hot mouth
swollen fire-tongue, vast inferno
supreme and immense
within this quivering space
that pulled it together
lifted it into place and hung it
like a bare bulb from a naked electric wire

Never The Breeze

The summers with their lofty grasses
and lengthy heat. A tangle of light
in the purity of lovemaking

Along the river always a slight wind
never the breeze stirs the cattails
and you in your creamy nakedness

above me like a downy bird
perched on a tall tower, in motion
with the river's deep music
and rippling grasses

In the distance, the beating wings of ducks
are the quickening of a pulse
landing and taking off
like one kiss after another

Slow Drain

The sun's hammer lifts its steel
drops its weight
and nails serious heat to the land
A child with too many fingers
touches the wings of an empty nest
a gray moth shimmers in black roses
I hold my arms open

they grow inside of me

knotted joints like desert stones

How is it you come to me
but not in body
where you take the shape
of a septic heart
I plug into your silence
close to your lips
listening for a whisper

that could dissolve this grief

I cannot stay in this sleep
where love is frozen and you
melt away knowingly willingly
There is need for opening my eyes
to see the distance peel farther
than I remember

Does it matter

that in this sleep I am falling
into the mouth a blind tunnel
that swallows me like a slow drain
and you like an octopus
clever and slippery

floating upwards backwards

away

Napa

Near the end of this dream
a moon shimmers in wet dust
on August rooftops

a spin of stones below me
earth thunders, rumbles, spills her guts

A clash of Venetian blinds
against a side of cold air

wakes me

The quake stepped heavily
on Napa
leaving debris like clay pieces
crushed beneath a stampede of wind

I am watching the stars
peck at the dark
my heart, uprooted
as if dying

(after a 3:30 AM, 6.1 earthquake)

Banjo Birds and Circles

Outside of the café
the muddled noise
from so much chatter
The color of the sky
is a blue circle
At the same time a woman
dressed as a hillbilly
strums a banjo in such a repetitive way
that each recurring chord is like
the metallic backwash of a sickness
The birds have stopped singing
out of fear
that the intrusive banjo is a predator
Abruptly a table of older men
erupts into extended laughter
The deformed banjo noise stops
The birds are singing again
and with hasty movements
the Hillbilly packs it in and moves on
and my eyes can do nothing
but follow her until she disappears

The color of the sky
is a blue circle The sun
is a yellow circle The café tables
are black circles And the birds
with their ancestral songs
are all that is needed to complete
this circle of beauty

Sardines Mesh and Scars

The freeway shakes with severe
nervousness. Bullets of light
ricochet then strike like livid eyes
The sun drops its broiled fruit
and cars mesh together
burning the air's thin garment
Faces in windows are dreams
that radiate and dissolve
Spinning tires run from death
anxious and burdened
Thick smears from treads are dark scars
on the road's body
Metal wheels burn with the furry
of a mass riot
Somebody's oil is leaking like black guts
from a belly wound Clashing music
breaks out of open windows
and everyone is compressed
like enormous cans of sardines
on a market shelf

Gate To The One Ending

At the marina near the water's edge
standing in a thicket of fog
like a piece of gray driftwood
a lean, elderly woman motions
the silence of Tai-Chi
separating slow movements
with moments of stationary shapes:
White Crane, Monkey, Cloud
and like long strands of pearls
undulating in the wind
many streaks of white hair
weave into the faded black
of her youth. At certain moments
she becomes a Chinese mime
living inside of herself.

In between the shore's rocks
lapping waves are filled with
harmonious lightness,
where each wave is caught
in a soft death, where, on the rocks,
spread-out seaweed becomes
a textile laid out to dry
and small shore birds peck at the green
as if seamstresses stitching fabric.

Beneath a sky of moist, dense gray
a discomforting low pressure
becomes the heaviness of sleep,
a disorientation, a punishment
that clogs my brain with a lead-like load,
with an atmospheric congestion
that mimes a head cold.

Sometimes I feel like a castaway
or an old pirate whose sword
has rounded to a useless edge
and life is unreal enough
to be misunderstood by
the numerous choices that lead
to one ending.

Standing a few yards behind the woman
I begin to mimic the circles and curves
of her slow motion practice:

maybe this is the way to be content,
to create a stance of fearlessness
at the gate to the one ending.

Nowhere To Be Found

As if praying, white clouds
cross blue sky's bright light,
a slither of breeze on a perch
In summer's width the air is hot
nearly still, glassy and free

The horizon's thin sepia haze
flickers, whistles, chips away at the blue
then dissolves into a valley of seaweed

Some footsteps implanted in the sand
a still life stranger, invisible passerby

A thunderous tumble of waves
a rumble, a torrent, a radiant slope
salt, thirst, sustenance

Born from this we have become
the bitter flavor, the dust, the haze
the churning stock of an unconscious arrival
Absorbed, consumed, immersed, we have become
agitated from outside in

where so few of us can hear our pulse
within its clear-cut vanishing. Stressed
jittery, so few of us can feel earth:
Primal Nest. Salvation.

When time brakes its last hour
the only expression left
will be speechlessness
and we will no nothing
not even ourselves

CODA

Earth

Earth, builder of beauty,
her plumb line: a still point,
precious center, damp minerals.

What I am composing are
earth-words: a swathe of heat,
painted deserts, morning's musk,
saguaro green.

Upon my lips, misted whispers,
a fog's low roots, daylight's glaze,
dawn's red vine, dappled light,
cypress, corn silk.

I shake my pen
and from its throat spills
night's ink sac: salt,
stones, spiced stars.

I shake it more. It empties
this imagery, my feelings,
black sand, spears of pine,
a slow river's steady stretch.

Earth pushes us from her womb
where an underground gurgle, like a god
blowing into a straw, creates air bubbles,
first breath, birth cry.

Like birds we build nests, lay eggs,
feel earth buzz in our bones:
a jug of dreams, seasons, necessities.

Acknowledgements

My gratitude to the following publications where these poems first appeared:

Lost Coast Review: "Yuba", "Nocturne in d-flat minor", "Eulogy For Roses", "The Moon's Deep Wounds", "Sweeping Heaven"

The Sandy River Review: "Harbor Scenes", "The Willowed Landscape", "Rain #2"

River & South Review: "Banjo Birds and Circles"

The Cape Rock: "Going Coastal"

Acumen Literary Journal (United Kingdom): "Invisible"

The Open Mouse (United Kingdom): "Appearance"

Stone Voices Magazine: "Gardener", "Mountains"

Diverse Voices Quarterly: "Dust", "Never The Breeze"

Eunoia Review (China): "Journey", "Nowhere To Be Found", "Earth", "Morning's Mirror"

Deep Tissue Magazine: "Some god", "Captivity", "Kleptomaniac", "We Are Only Sleeping", "Fallen Sea Star"

The Muse (India): "Scenes From Cedar Park"

Miracle Magazine: "Full Life In The Day Of A Poet", "The Sound Of Bones"

Literature Today (India): "Raven"

Red Wolf Press: "Urgency"

Poetry Pacific (Canada): "Naked Cry", "Corrosion"

Rose Red Review: "A Dream Held In A Mouth"

Jellyfish Whispers: "Enchanted", "Solo Flight"

Calliope Magazine: "Journals"

Empty Sink Publishing: "Hypnotize The Beast", "A Far-Flung Future", "Circle"

Metaphor Magazine (Philippines): "In The Body Of A Daydream", "Spring, A Birthing Womb"

Dead Snakes Journal: "Queen", "Lead and Salt", "Sardines Mesh and Scars"

Digital Papercut: "Time Is Nothing When It Is Dark", "Napa", "Teachers", "City Portrait", "The Bird Flew Off"

Orion headless: "Rattle"

KNOT Magazine: "The Translator", "Wildcat Canyon"

The Filid Anthology: "Nocturne"

Berkeley Times: "Gate To The One Ending"

Words & Images In Flight: "Embrace"

Poetry Super Highway.com: "Sun" (poem of the week)

Thank You to Poet Elina Petrova for her insightful Foreword.

Also, I wish to express my appreciation to these members of the poetry critique group 'The Poet's Lounge': Paul Larner, Heather M. Browne, Lotta Hellron, Kerri Rochell, Diana Baker-Vevang, Chad Repko, Munia Kahn and Stephen Edward Godfrey, whom, in countless ways, shaped many of these poems from draft to finish with their excellent suggestions and sincere writers camaraderie. Thank you.

My deepest gratitude to Editor-in-Chief, Dustin Pickering, and to Assistant Editor, Z. M. Wise, of 'Transcendent Zero Press', for selecting 'The Translator' for book publication. Thank you for your warmhearted welcome, and for your masterful treatment of 'The Translator' from manuscript to published book. Pickering and Wise are the stars.

Last and surely not least, thank you to Dustin Pickering, Heather M. Browne, Munia Khan, and Eve Costello, for their back cover statements.

NOTE: "Solo Flight" was also published in 'Storm Cycle Anthology Best Of 2014" (Kind Of A Hurricane Press), and in 'Metaphor Magazine'.

"Going Coastal" was also published in 'Metaphor Magazine'.

Author

Born April 7th, 1950 in Herkimer, New York, along the Mohawk River, near the foothills of the Adirondack Mountains, and raised in Ilion, New York (just across the river), Dah has been a resident of Berkeley, California since 1980 where for the past fifteen years he has been teaching 'Chakra Four Yoga' to children and adults.

A prolific writer, a musician, and an awarding-winning photographer, Dah has been writing poetry for five decades, and according to himself, he has not reached the degree of writing that he knows exists somewhere in his mind. He is simultaneously working on his fifth and sixth manuscripts.

Between 2013 and 2014, 76 of Dah's poems were published in 36 reviews, journals and magazines by editors from the United States, the United Kingdom, Canada, India, the Philippines and China which also includes his essay "Grandmother" published in 'Estuary Magazine'.

Dah along with U.K. Poet, Paul Larner created 'The Poet's Lounge', a small Facebook poetry critique group/workshop that has motivated the growth of dozens of aspiring and accomplished poets, with members from India, Sweden, the Philippines, the U.K. and the U.S.

Visit Dah's 'Words Of Dahlusion'
https://dahlusion.wordpress.com

Email: dahlusion@yahoo.com

Books by Dah

The Translator (2015)

If You Have One Moment (2015)

The Second Coming (2012)

In Forbidden Language (2010)

'The Translator' Cover Design © Dah 2015

Cover Photograph: Sunset, Death Valley © Dah 2007

See more of Dah's photography at: www.flickr.com/photos/dahlusion

Google: dahlusion

www.ingramcontent.com/pod-product-compliance
Lightning Source LLC
LaVergne TN
LVHW051657080426
835511LV00017B/2611